OUR DAILY BREAD FOR KIDS™

Meaningful Moments with God

Written by
Crystal Bowman & Teri McKinley

Illustrated by Luke Flowers

Discovery House®
from Our Daily Bread Ministries

To my mom, Gerene Langejans,
a servant of Jesus who has proclaimed His love to the next generation.
—C.B.

In loving memory of my father-in-law, Terry McKinley,
who wanted all people to know Jesus.
—T.M.

To Owen, Lydia, and Naomi, my little lights that shine brightly with the love of the Lord.
May you continue to grow brighter with His Word.
—L.F.

With special thanks to Andrew, Paul, Miranda, Kris,
and the Discovery House team for their excellent work.

Our Daily Bread for Kids
© 2014 by Crystal Bowman and Teri McKinley
Illustrations © 2014 Luke Flowers
All rights reserved.

Discovery House is affiliated with Our Daily Bread Ministries, Grand Rapids, Michigan.

Requests for permission to quote from this book should be directed to:
Permissions Department, Discovery House Publishers, P.O. Box 3566, Grand Rapids, MI 49501,
or contact us by e-mail at permissionsdept@dhp.org

Design by Kris Nelson/StoryLook Design

Library of Congress Cataloging-in-Publication Data
Bowman, Crystal.
    Our daily bread for kids : 365 meaningful moments with God /
Crystal Bowman and Teri McKinley ; illustrations by Luke Flowers.
        p.   cm
    ISBN 978-1-62707-332-5
    1. Devotional calendars--Juvenile literature. I. Flowers, Luke, illustrator. II. Title.
BV4870.B6955 2014
242'.62--dc23   2014037748

Printed in the United States of America
First printing in 2014

INTRODUCTION

One day Jesus' disciples asked Him how they should pray. Jesus taught them a prayer that has become famous all over the world. It's often called **"The Lord's Prayer."** This is how Jesus prayed:

"Our Father in heaven,

hallowed be your name, your kingdom come,

your will be done, on earth as it is in heaven.

Give us today our daily bread.

And forgive us our debts,

as we also have forgiven our debtors.

And lead us not into temptation,

but deliver us from the evil one."

MATTHEW 6:9–13 NIV

Did you notice those three words, **"our daily bread"**? What do they mean?

Throughout the Bible God shows that He loves people by taking care of their needs every day. One of our biggest needs is food—actual bread for our bodies and spiritual "bread" for our souls. God fed His chosen people, the Israelites, by sending bread called manna to their campsites every morning. In the New Testament, Jesus calls himself our "bread of life."

This book is all about our spiritual food. The readings in Our Daily Bread for Kids will help you get inside the Bible every day. They were written to explain Bible stories and ideas, and they will always point you to what God says in Scripture. Every day you can read one of these devotionals and your Bible.

If Scripture is the bread that feeds our souls, this book is like the plate that serves the bread. Keep it right next to your Bible!

This is not a Bible storybook, so the readings do not follow the order of Scripture. Some readings are about Jesus or other people in the New Testament, some are about stories from the Old Testament, and some are about Bible verses that might have a special meaning for you. If you come across anything you don't understand, just keep reading. Don't give up! The more you read and study the Bible, the more you will understand the big story God has for us.

You can read this book by yourself, or have your parents or grandparents read it with you. You might want to use this book at mealtime or at bedtime. However you use Our Daily Bread for Kids, we hope you like it. But more importantly, we hope you learn that Jesus loves you so much that He's given you a chance to become a part of God's family.

As you use this book, we pray you will have many meaningful moments with God.

Crystal and Teri

A Special Creation

Then the LORD God
formed a man. He
made him out of the
dust of the ground.
He breathed the
breath of life into him.
And the man became
a living person.

GENESIS 2:7 NIRV

In the beginning there was nothing but water and darkness. The earth was empty. It had no shape. But God was there before everything else, and He had a plan to create a world.

God is so powerful that all He had to do was speak to fill the world with good things. First He said, "Let there be light." And there was light. Then He told the water to separate from the sky—so it did. Then God said, "Let the waters be gathered into one place." And that is exactly what happened. God told trees and plants to appear on the land—so they did. Then God created the sun, moon, and stars and put them in the sky. He told birds to fly in the sky and fish to swim in the seas. God told the land to bring forth different kinds of animals—and it did. God liked everything He made because it was good.

I am created by God.

On the last day of creation, God decided to make a man. But God didn't say, "Let there be a man." Instead of using words, God did something different. He formed a man from the dust of the earth. Then God breathed His own breath into the man, and the man became a living person.

People are different from the rest of God's creation. He made us so we can talk to Him, love Him, and know Him in a real and personal way. God created you and gave life to you too. You are a special part of His creation, just like the first person He created.
—C.B.

READ MORE

Read Genesis 2:21–22.
Who was the second person God created?
How did God create her?

FUN FACT

Did you know that
water covers most of
the earth? Only about
one-fourth of the
earth is dry land.

Can You See It?

> Ever since the world was created it has been possible to see the qualities of God that are not seen. I'm talking about his eternal power and about the fact that he is God. Those things can be seen in what he has made.
>
> **ROMANS 1:20 NIRV**

You cannot see the wind, but you can see what it does. You can watch trees wave back and forth as the wind blows their branches. You can watch a boat glide across a lake as the wind pushes its sails. You can watch a kite soar high into the sky as the wind carries it along. And you can watch an umbrella turn inside out on a windy, rainy day. If someone said, "I don't believe in the wind because I cannot see it," that would be silly. We know the wind is real because we can see everything it does.

Just like the wind, we can't see God either—but we can see what He does. We can look at the nighttime sky and see the moon and stars He created. We can see His power in the waves of a mighty ocean. We can watch a flock of geese fly south for the winter as God guides them along. And we can see His artwork when He paints colorful sunsets and rainbows.

God wants us to know He is real. That is why He reveals himself to us through His creation. If you want to see God, just look around at all He does. God's work is everywhere! —C.B.

I can see what God does everywhere.

FUN FACT

The strongest hurricanes, called "Category 5," have winds over 155 miles an hour. That's more than twice as fast as cars on the highway.

READ MORE

What does Psalm 19:1–6 tell us about God's creation?

Just Ask!

Kids who get the best grades in school often win awards. It is good to study hard and be smart, but it is also important to be wise.

A person who is smart knows many things. But a person who is wise knows how to make good choices. Wise people understand how to treat others with kindness and respect. They understand what is right and wrong. They choose to live the way God wants them to.

> If any of you needs wisdom, you should ask God for it. God is generous. He enjoys giving to all people, so God will give you wisdom.
> **JAMES 1:5 ICB**

The Old Testament tells us about a wise man named Solomon. He became king of Israel after his father, David, passed away. God spoke to Solomon in a dream and said He would give Solomon whatever he wanted. Many people would ask for money or popularity or a long life. But Solomon asked for wisdom. God was very pleased with that choice. God told Solomon that because he asked for wisdom, he would also get riches and honor.

Ask God for wisdom.

God will give me wisdom. All I need to do is ask.

In the New Testament, James tells us that if we ask God for wisdom He will give it to us. Many times, we get wisdom from God's Word, the Bible. When we read the Bible, God helps us to understand what is right and wrong. He helps us understand how He wants us to live.

You don't have to be grown-up to be wise. You can ask God for wisdom right now. It's a wise thing to do! —C.B.

READ MORE
**Read Proverbs 2:1–11.
What are the rewards of wisdom?**

FUN FACT
The word *wisdom* appears in the Bible more than two hundred times.

> He will cover you
> with his wings.
> Under the feathers
> of his wings you
> will find safety.
> He is faithful.
> He will keep you
> safe like a shield
> or a tower.
>
> **PSALM 91:4 NIRV**

Wings of Safety

A mother hen is very protective of her chicks. She begins to care for her babies when they are just eggs. She pays close attention to the eggs' temperature. She pecks at other birds or animals that come near the nest. When the chicks finally break out of their eggshells, the mother hen continues to watch them carefully. Any time the hen senses danger, she makes a clucking noise and spreads her wings. The babies run underneath her wings to hide. There the chicks are safe and warm. They can even walk around underneath the shelter of their mother's wings.

I can run to God when I am in danger.

Psalm 91 says that God protects you like a mother hen protects her chicks. When you think of God guarding you, imagine a hen spreading her wings. When you are afraid, God wants you to run to Him for safety. You can always depend on Him to be your shelter.

But how do we run to God? We can run to Him anytime by praying to Him and asking Him to help us.

Whether it's daytime or nighttime, you can stay close to God. When you are close to Him, God covers you with His wings of safety. —T.M.

FUN FACT

A hen's wings stretch twenty to thirty inches (fifty-one to seventy-six centimeters). That means about twelve chicks can fit under her wings at one time.

READ MORE

Read Psalm 17:8.
Use this as a prayer asking God to keep you safe.

Dinner on the Mountainside

Imagine trying to feed five thousand people. That would take a lot of food!

The Bible says Jesus fed five thousand hungry people on a mountainside. And that number doesn't even include the women and children who were there! There wasn't a store on the mountain where Jesus could buy food. There wasn't a barn full of food nearby. But there was a young boy in the crowd who had five small loaves of bread and two little fish. And he was willing to share with Jesus.

> Then Jesus took the loaves and gave thanks. He handed out the bread to those who were seated. He gave them as much as they wanted. And he did the same with the fish.
>
> **JOHN 6:11 NIRV**

Jesus' disciples didn't think the boy's lunch would help thousands of hungry people. But Jesus performed a miracle. First He told the people to sit down. Then He thanked God for the food and began to hand it out. He turned a small lunch into a huge dinner for all those people! There were even leftovers for the disciples.

Jesus can use what I have, no matter how big or small.

The Bible doesn't tell us the name of the boy. We don't know anything else about him. It seems he was a regular kid. But Jesus showed His own greatness because a boy was willing to share the small amount he had.

Like that boy, we all can give what we have. It doesn't matter what it is. What matters is that we are willing to share what we have with others.

When you give, Jesus can do great things through you too. —T.M.

READ MORE

Did you know God performed a similar miracle in the Old Testament? Read about it in 2 Kings 4:42–44.

FUN FACT

The average loaf of bread has about twenty slices. Without Jesus' miracle, it would have taken around 250 loaves of bread just to give everyone in the crowd a single slice.

> Two people are better than one. They can help each other in everything they do.
>
> **ECCLESIASTES 4:9 NIRV**

Let's Work Together

It's fun to play catch on a sunny afternoon. But have you ever tried to play catch by yourself? It is not very easy to do alone! You need a friend to catch the ball when you throw it. And you need someone to throw the ball back when it's your turn to catch.

Chores might not be as much fun as playing catch. But have you noticed that chores are easier with two people? Making a bed by yourself can take a long time. Straightening the sheets and fluffing the pillows is a lot of work! But with another person's help, you can get the work done much more quickly.

The Bible says two people can do more together than one person alone. It is good to remember this when we serve God too. Just as playing catch and doing chores are better with friends, Christians accomplish more when they work together. And remember that God is the one who gives you the strength to work!

Think about all the people you see serving at church. The pastor preaches a message to the people, but many others serve too. Sunday school teachers, greeters, musicians, and other helpers all work as a team so people can worship together and learn about God.

Two are better than one.

Can you think of ways you can work with others at home, at church, or at school? You will get more done and have more fun! —T.M.

FUN FACT

The world record for one person running a mile is three minutes and forty-three seconds. But the world record for a relay team running the same distance is much better—only two minutes and fifty-four seconds!

READ MORE

Read Mark 6:7.
How did Jesus send out His disciples?

A Big Assignment

God created a perfect world. But when people disobeyed God, they ruined His perfect world. The people were sinful and didn't care about God. God was sorry that He had made people to live on the earth. He wanted to start over.

Noah did everything exactly as God commanded him.
GENESIS 6:22 NIRV

But there was one man who still loved God, and his name was Noah. God had a big assignment for Noah!

God told Noah to build a giant boat—called an ark—big enough for his family, two of every animal, and lots and lots of food. Noah would build the ark of cypress wood and cover it with tar inside and out. It was big—450 feet long (about 137 meters), 75 feet wide (about 23 meters), and 45 feet high (about 14 meters). God told Noah that He was going to send a flood to destroy the earth, but He would keep Noah and his family safe inside the ark.

God wants me to obey Him, even when others don't.

The Bible doesn't say how long it took Noah to build the ark, but it may have taken a hundred years! Some people probably laughed at Noah for building the ark. But Noah did everything God told him to do because he trusted God. When the flood came, Noah and his family were safe in the ark while the rest of the world was destroyed.

It's not always easy to obey God. It may be hard if your friends are not doing the right things. They might even laugh. But God is pleased when you let Him work through you. And He may even give you a big assignment someday! —C.B.

READ MORE

Read Genesis 8:6–12. How did Noah know the flood water was finally going down?

FUN FACT

The world's largest ship today is called the *Prelude*. It is 1,601 feet long (488 meters), more than three times the length of Noah's ark!

Amazing and Wonderful

> How you made me is amazing and wonderful. I praise you for that. What you have done is wonderful. I know that very well. . . . God, your thoughts about me are priceless. No one can possibly add them all up.
>
> **PSALM 139:14, 17 NIRV**

Did you know that no two snowflakes are exactly alike? Each snowflake has its own special pattern and design. The same is true for people—not even identical twins are alike in every way.

Every person God creates is unique. That means there is no one else exactly like you. From your laugh to your freckles to the color of your hair—God made you, and He knows all about you.

Think about the things you like to do and the things you're really good at. Not only does God know your interests and talents, He's the one who gave them to you. He thought about you before you were even born. He planned your smile and the color of your eyes. He knew what would make you laugh and what subjects you would like in school. He gave you your own voice and your own personality.

I am a wonderful part of God's creation.

Every part of God's creation—including you—is amazing and wonderful! In the book of Psalms, King David thanks God for making him in such an amazing and wonderful way. He praises God for thinking about him so much.

David says that God's thoughts about him are priceless. God's thoughts about you are priceless too. You have great value because God made you amazing and wonderful. —T.M.

FUN FACT

Your fingerprints are unique to you. They are on your fingers when you're born, and stay the same throughout your whole life.

READ MORE

Read Psalm 139:1–6. What does God know about you?

Kids Can Make a Difference

There are many kings in the Bible—some were good, and others were very bad. The Bible tells us that King Josiah was one of the best. He did what was right in the eyes of God.

The Bible says something very interesting about Josiah. Are you ready for this? He was only eight years old when he became king! Josiah had some adult helpers, of course, but he was the leader.

Some of the kings before Josiah were evil, and God's people began worshipping other gods which weren't even real. Josiah knew that was wrong! So when he was twenty-six years old he destroyed all the places where people worshipped other gods. He got rid of the statues of the fake gods the people had made. Josiah took away everything else the Lord hated in the land. That was a big job for a young king, but he did it because he loved God, and he wanted the people to love God too.

> There was no king like Josiah either before him or after him. None of them turned to the LORD as he did. He followed the LORD with all his heart and all his soul. He followed him with all his strength. He did everything the Law of Moses required.
>
> **2 KINGS 23:25 NIRV**

I can make a difference no matter how old I am.

Have you ever thought you're too young to make a difference? That's not true. There are many things that kids can do to serve God. Maybe you could be a friend to a lonely kid at school or in your neighborhood. Maybe you could invite other kids to church or Sunday school so they can learn more about God. By being a good friend, you can make a difference in another person's life.

With God's help, you can make a difference—even if you're not a king! —C.B.

READ MORE

King Josiah promised to do something very important. Read 2 Kings 23:1–3 to find out what it was.

FUN FACT

Alfonso XIII of Spain was declared king as soon as he was born in 1886.

Fix your thoughts on what is true, and honorable, and right, and pure, and lovely, and admirable. Think about things that are excellent and worthy of praise.

PHILIPPIANS 4:8 NLT

God is good!

Something to Think About

What do you think about when you go for a walk? How blue the sky is? How the sun feels on your face? Why the squirrels run away as you get close to them? God loves it when we think about good things.

But thinking those good thoughts can be hard when bad things happen around us. And bad things do happen. Kids have problems just like grown-ups do. That's why God tells everyone to think about things that are good and worthy of praise. He wants us to remember that He is in control. He wants us to trust Him and believe that He will take care of us.

When I think about good things, I will thank God.

Today's Bible verse says to think about what is "true, and honorable, and right." Things like this: God loves you and cares about you. God wants what is best for you. God has a special plan for your life. God will always be with you.

The verse also says to think about what is "pure, and lovely, and admirable." You could think about pure snowflakes and lovely butterflies. You could think about the people in your life who you admire.

When you do something nice for another person, don't you enjoy being thanked? So does God! Thank Him for giving you so many good things to think about.
—C.B.

FUN FACT

Our brains think anywhere from twelve thousand to fifty thousand thoughts every day!

READ MORE
What does Psalm 105:1–8 tell us to do?

Why Me, God?

Moses was an Israelite. That means he was one of God's special people. One day, when he was guarding a flock of sheep, Moses saw a bush that was burning with fire. But it never burned up! So Moses walked over for a closer look.

Suddenly God's voice came from the bush. "Moses, Moses," God said. "Take off your sandals for you are standing on very special ground."

But Moses said to God, "Who am I that I should go to Pharaoh and bring the people of Israel out of Egypt?"

EXODUS 3:11 GW

God told Moses that He had heard the cries of the Israelites, who were living in Egypt as slaves. God wanted Moses to lead His people out of Egypt. But Moses didn't think he was the right person for the job.

Moses gave God all kinds of excuses. But God kept telling Moses that He would help. God even showed Moses miracles to prove His power. Still, Moses tried to say "no."

I will say "yes" to God when He wants to use me.

"I'm not a good speaker," Moses said.

"I will help you speak," God told him.

Finally, Moses told God to send someone else! Moses was looking at his own weakness rather than God's power. God could have taken His people out of Egypt by himself, but He wanted to use Moses for the job.

You know what? God still uses people to do His work. Whenever God chooses people, He gives them the ability to do the job He has for them. When we say "yes" to God, He will do great things through us. —C.B.

READ MORE

Moses became a great leader for the children of Israel. Read Exodus 14:10–31. How did God use Moses in this story?

FUN FACT

"Burning bush" is the name of a shrub that turns fiery red and orange in the fall. The shrub got its name from the Bible story.

What Is God Like?

> The LORD your God . . .
> is gracious. He is
> tender and kind.
> He is slow to get
> angry. He is full
> of love. He takes
> pity on you.
>
> JOEL 2:13 NIRV

Video chats are fun. It's great to be able to see and hear a person who lives far away. Maybe you have a relative or friend in another city, or even another country. With the right computer or phone, you can see that person's smile and hear her laugh!

When you can see and hear someone else, it's easier to know what that person is like. Being face-to-face makes you feel closer to others.

But you can't see God face-to-face, and He doesn't talk to you out loud. Sometimes you might wonder what God is like, or feel like He's far away. That's why He gave us the Bible. His Word shows us what He is like.

The Bible says God is loving and cares about you. He is tender and gentle. God is kind. He doesn't get angry easily. God loves you a lot. He understands how you feel when you are sad or having a bad day. Everything about God is good.

You can't talk to God over video chat. But when you want to know more about Him, your Bible will tell you everything you need to know. The verses you read will help you understand just what God is like. —T.M.

Reading the Bible will help me know about God.

FUN FACT

The telephone company AT&T created a "Picturephone" as early as 1964.

READ MORE

What does Micah 7:19 tell us about God?

Moving Day

> But Ruth replied, "Don't try to make me leave you and go back. Where you go I'll go. Where you stay I'll stay. Your people will be my people. Your God will be my God."
>
> **RUTH 1:16 NIRV**

Moving can be scary! Whether you move to a new school or church or city, it can be difficult to make new friends. It might be hard to find where you need to go. And everything is just different. Sometimes people have to move even when they don't really want to.

The Bible tells the story of a woman named Ruth, who chose to move—even though she didn't have to. Ruth was from a country called Moab. She met her husband when his family came to Moab in search of food. There was a famine—a time when food is hard to find—in their hometown of Bethlehem.

Ruth lived with her husband and his family in Moab for ten years, but then something terrible happened. All the men in the family died! Ruth's husband, his brother, and the men's father were gone. Three women were on their own. Ruth's mother-in-law, Naomi, decided to move back to Bethlehem. She hoped God would help her there.

Wherever I go, I know God will be with me.

Ruth's sister-in-law, Orpah, went to her own family in Moab, but Ruth followed Naomi. Ruth left the place she had always lived to go to Naomi's town. Naomi told Ruth to stay in Moab. She even tried to talk Ruth out of going to Bethlehem.

But Ruth knew it was right to help her mother-in-law, so she moved anyway. Because of Ruth's courage, God blessed both women. He provided food for them and gave Ruth a new husband.

Before long, Ruth had a baby—and that baby became the grandfather of King David!

Ruth's story shows that God will be with us wherever we go. If you ever have to go somewhere new, remember this: God will go with you. —T.M.

READ MORE

Read Genesis 12:1–4.
Who did God tell to move to another country?

FUN FACT

In the Hebrew language, the name *Bethlehem* means "house of bread."

Marked by the Owner

> [God] put his Spirit in our hearts and marked us as his own. We can now be sure that he will give us everything he promised us.
>
> **2 CORINTHIANS 1:22 NIRV**

If you ever see a cow up close, you might notice some letters or a colored tag on its body. A farmer will often put a mark on his animals. He does this to show that the animals belong to him. Farmers choose a special way of marking their animals that is different from the other farmers' marks. Then, if the animal gets lost, it can be returned to its owner. Everyone knows who the animal belongs to because of its mark.

Did you know the Bible says God marks people too? You can't see the mark, but it's there. The Bible tells us that when we believe in Jesus the Holy Spirit comes into our hearts. The Holy Spirit is God's mark on us. It means we belong to Jesus!

When we belong to Jesus, we receive all of God's promises. He will be with us. He will protect us. He will provide for us. He takes care of His people, just like a farmer watches over his animals.

Once we ask Jesus to forgive our sins, we will always be His. No one can ever take His love away from us or pull us away from Him. Even if the world seems scary, Jesus is watching over everyone who carries His mark. —T.M.

Jesus marks those who belong to Him.

FUN FACT

The ancient Egyptians were probably the first people to mark their animals.

READ MORE

Read Ephesians 1:13.
How does this verse explain how Christians are marked?

Daniel Prayed Anyway

Have you ever heard the story of Daniel and the lions' den? Do you know why Daniel spent a night with the lions?

Daniel was a man who lived far from home. He worked in the palace of a king named Darius. The king wanted to put Daniel in charge of everything because Daniel was trustworthy. The other men who worked with Daniel were jealous and wanted to get rid of him.

Daniel was faithful to God. Three times each day, he went to his room and prayed to God. Daniel's enemies tricked Darius into signing a law that said everyone had to pray to the king. If anyone prayed to someone else, that person would be thrown into a den of lions.

> When Daniel heard that the new law had been written, he went to his house. He went to his upstairs room. The windows of that room opened toward Jerusalem. Three times each day Daniel got down on his knees and prayed. He prayed and thanked God, just as he always had done.
>
> DANIEL 6:10 ICB

When Daniel heard about the law, he continued to pray to God three times a day, just like before. Though Daniel worked for King Darius, he worshipped God. So Daniel prayed only to God—and no law was going to change that.

The lions' den was dangerous, but Daniel trusted God. When Daniel was thrown into the den, God kept him safe by sending an angel to shut the lions' mouths.

Praying to God is always the right thing to do.

Some people don't want us to pray, but we can pray anyway. It doesn't have to be out loud. You don't have to get on your knees. You can pray in your mind and in your heart. You can be faithful to God just like Daniel was! —C.B.

READ MORE
King Darius made another law.
Read Daniel 6:26–27 to find out what it was.

FUN FACT
A grown-up male lion eats about fifteen pounds of meat per day. That would be sixty quarter-pound hamburgers!

> "As long as the earth lasts, there will always be a time to plant and a time to gather the crops. As long as the earth lasts, there will always be cold and heat. There will always be summer and winter, day and night."
>
> **GENESIS 8:22 NIRV**

Always the Same

When you wake up in the morning and see the sun, you know it's the beginning of a new day. You know it will be light for many hours. When you go to bed at night, you know it will be dark for a long time so you can sleep. Then it will be morning again. You never wake up in the morning to find out that it's suddenly nighttime.

The same is true of the seasons. Though seasons change, they always follow the same order. Spring always follows winter, and summer always comes after spring. Fall always follows summer, and winter always comes after fall. It would be crazy if one year fall came after winter, or summer followed fall. Farmers wouldn't be able to plant their crops or harvest them at the right time. Birds wouldn't know when to fly north or south for the season!

God always stays the same.

God is a God of order. He created the sun and moon to mark the days and seasons. The earth obeys His orders, and that will never change. God never changes either. You can always count on Him to be with you.

When you wake up in the morning, God is there—just like the sun. When you go to bed at night, God is with you—all through the hours of darkness. Every hour, every day, every season, every year, God loves you. And that will never change. —C.B.

FUN FACT

One of the hottest days on earth was July 10, 1913, when it was 134° F (56.7° C) in Furnace Creek, California. One of the coldest days ever was July 20, 1983, when it was −128.6° F (−89.2° C) in Antarctica.

READ MORE
Read Hebrews 13:8.
What does this verse tell us about Jesus?

Best Buddies

Having a best friend is special. It's more fun to play hide-and-seek with someone you like. It's nice to have a friend to build a fort with. Eating ice cream is even sweeter when you can share it with a friend. God gives friendship as a gift. And He can use it to do great things!

> Jonathan and David became close friends. Jonathan loved David just as he loved himself.
>
> **1 SAMUEL 18:1 NIRV**

The Bible tells us about two best friends. Their names were David and Jonathan. Jonathan was the son of Saul, the first king of Israel. Saul liked Jonathan's friend David for a while, but then he became jealous. Saul knew that David was going to be the next king—and he wasn't happy about that. Saul tried to keep David from becoming king and even tried to hurt David.

Friendship is a gift from God.

But no matter what, Jonathan was loyal to David. Even though Jonathan could have been the next king, he never became jealous of David. Jonathan talked honestly with David and helped him escape when Saul wanted to hurt him. The Bible says Jonathan "loved David just as he loved himself." That means he did what was best for David, even when it was hard.

Jonathan is a great example of a good friend, just like Jesus is a good example for us. A good friend helps out and puts his friends' feelings ahead of his own. At church, at school, and in your neighborhood, you can show God's love by being a good friend!
—T.M.

READ MORE
Read 1 Samuel 19:4.
What did Jonathan tell King Saul to do?

FUN FACT
The name *David* means "loved." David was loved by his friend Jonathan.

Beautiful Feet

It is written,
"How beautiful are
the feet of those who
bring good news!"
ROMANS 10:15 NIRV

Feet are not always pleasant. They can be sweaty and stinky! When you walk outside without shoes your feet can be covered in dust or sticky mud.

But the Bible says people who take the good news about Jesus to others have beautiful feet. It doesn't matter what their feet look like—or even how they smell. Feet can be beautiful because they carry people out to preach the good news about Jesus.

A missionary is a person with beautiful feet. Missionaries have a special job because they tell others about God's love. They tell others about God's Son, Jesus. Did you know you can be a missionary right now? You can take God's Word to people right where you are! People all around you are ready to hear about Jesus.

Maybe you have family members who are still learning about God. Maybe you have a friend at school who wants to know more about the Bible. You can teach them and encourage them to love Jesus. You can take the good news about Jesus to anyone. It doesn't matter how old you are or where you go. When you tell other people about God, your feet are beautiful! —T.M.

My beautiful feet take me to tell others about God.

FUN FACT

Some health experts say people should try to take ten thousand steps per day. That means you would walk about 115,000 miles in a lifetime!

READ MORE

To read a Bible story about feet, look up John 13:1–17.

Lots of Names

Do you know why your parents chose your name? Some kids are given a name because of what the name means. Sometimes they're named after someone else in their family. And sometimes they're given a name just because their parents like it. Our first name is usually what people call us, and our last name tells others what family we belong to. Names are important!

The prophet Isaiah lived a long time before Jesus was born. But he wrote down many special names for Jesus. God told Isaiah about things that were going to happen in the future. The prophet wrote those things down in the Old Testament book of Isaiah. One thing Isaiah wrote was that God's Son would be born as a baby.

> For a child is born to us, a son is given to us. The government will rest on his shoulders. And he will be called: Wonderful Counselor, Mighty God, Everlasting Father, Prince of Peace.
>
> **ISAIAH 9:6 NLT**

Jesus has many wonderful names.

About seven hundred years later, an angel visited a girl named Mary and told her she was going to be the mother of God's Son. The angel told Mary to name her baby Jesus.

But Isaiah had said that Jesus would be called by other names too. People would call him "Wonderful Counselor" because He would be a teacher of truth. They would call Him "Mighty God" because He would have God's power. He would be called "Everlasting Father" because He came from His Father in heaven and would live forever. He would be called "Prince of Peace" because He would bring peace to everyone who believes in Him as Savior. Jesus has many special names because He is the most special person of all!
—C.B.

READ MORE

In Matthew 16:13–16, Jesus asked one of His disciples who people thought He was. How did Peter answer Jesus?

FUN FACT

Since the year 912, there have been forty-seven kings and world rulers named Henry!

> He remembers
> his covenant forever,
> the promise he made,
> for a thousand
> generations.
>
> **PSALM 105:8 NIV**

Promises, Promises

God gives us a lot of promises in the Bible. Some of them can be found in the Old Testament, and others are in the New Testament. We don't know for sure how many promises are in the Bible, but some people have counted more than three thousand!

What kinds of promises does God make? He promises to take care of us and watch over us. He promises to give us what we need. He promises to comfort us when we're sad. He promises to lead us and guide us if we ask Him to. He promises to help us with our troubles. He promises to give us wisdom and power. He promises to listen when we pray to Him. God doesn't promise that our lives will be easy—but He promises that He will always be with us. The best promise of all is that we can live forever with Him when we believe in Jesus as our Savior.

God keeps His promises.

People make promises too. But people don't always keep their promises. Sometimes we forget what we had promised. Sometimes we find that other people or things get in the way. And even though it's wrong, sometimes we just change our minds.

But God is never like that. He doesn't forget. He doesn't get confused. He doesn't change His mind. God does what He says He will do. He will always keep His promises—all three thousand of them! —C.B.

FUN FACT
Other words with meanings similar to "promise" are covenant, pledge, vow, and oath.

READ MORE
Read Matthew 28:20.
What promise did Jesus give to His disciples before going back to heaven?

Prayer Power

Prayer is talking to God. We can pray to thank God for our dinner. We can pray to tell God when we're sad or scared. We can pray to ask God for things we need.

So Peter was kept in prison. But the church prayed hard to God for him.

ACTS 12:5 NIRV

Prayer can be powerful. Sometimes when we pray, God will do things that seem impossible.

After Jesus was taken to heaven, Peter and the other disciples were telling everyone about Him. The king didn't like that. He arrested some of the disciples and did terrible things to them. Then he arrested Peter and put him in prison. While Peter waited to learn what the king would do to him, the church was praying hard for Peter. And God heard their prayers.

In the middle of the night, Peter was sleeping between two soldiers. He had chains around his wrists. Suddenly, an angel appeared. "Hurry!" the angel said. "Get up!" And guess what? The chains fell off Peter's arms!

My prayers are powerful.

The angel led Peter out of prison. Peter was so confused he didn't think what was happening was real. But it was real. The angel walked Peter past the guards and led him to the city gate. The big metal gate opened all by itself! Once Peter was safe, the angel left, and Peter realized he was not having a dream. So he went to the house where his friends were praying. They were amazed when he told them what happened.

No matter what you pray about, God hears you. Sometimes, He answers in amazing ways! —T.M.

READ MORE

Did you know this wasn't the only time God sent an angel to rescue people from prison? Read Acts 5:17–20 to discover another time God helped His followers.

FUN FACT

Many cities in Bible times were protected by thick walls. A city gate was an opening in the wall that could be closed at night to keep out enemies.

> The LORD and King gives me strength. He makes my feet like the feet of a deer. He helps me walk on the highest places.
>
> **HABAKKUK 3:19 NIRV**

Run like a Deer

Did you know that deer can take their first steps about half an hour after they're born? At first, their legs are wobbly, but when deer are grown, they can run very fast and jump very high.

A deer's long legs are built for strength and speed. Because they can run fast and jump high, deer can often escape other animals that try to attack them. When a deer runs at high speed, it can leap over fallen trees or large rocks. Deer are also graceful animals with good balance. They can walk on steep rocks and hills without stumbling.

In the Bible, a prophet named Habakkuk used the example of deer to help us understand that God is our strength. When we love God and spend time learning more about Him, He gives us the strength we need to run away from trouble. When we get our strength from God and His Word, He will keep us from stumbling into sin.

Sometimes kids can find themselves in hard situations. If someone wants you to do something that you know is wrong, imagine a deer running at high speed. Just say no. Turn and walk away from that temptation. God can give you strength to run from danger and find a place that is safe. —C.B.

God will help me to run from danger.

FUN FACT

White-tailed deer can run at a top speed of about thirty-six miles per hour (about fifty-eight kilometers per hour). They can jump about eight feet high (about two and a half meters) and thirty feet long (about nine meters).

READ MORE

Psalm 42:1 is another verse about deer. What does this verse says about being thirsty?

Even though you
planned evil
against me, God
planned good
to come out of it.

GENESIS 50:20 GW

Good Instead of Bad

Joseph had eleven brothers. Their father, Jacob, liked Joseph best and gave him a colorful coat.

Joseph's brothers were jealous of him. They were mean and they picked on him. One day when all the brothers were in a field, they decided to get rid of Joseph for good. They met some travelers passing by and sold Joseph to be their slave. Joseph's brothers thought they would never see him again. But they were wrong.

Even though Joseph's brothers did mean things to him, God was with Joseph. He helped Joseph succeed in everything he did. After a few years, Joseph became an important official in Egypt!

God told Joseph that Egypt was going to run out of food. He gave Joseph wisdom to prepare for the famine so that all the Egyptians would have enough to eat.

When others are unkind, I know God is in control.

When the famine came, Joseph's brothers traveled to Egypt to buy food. They didn't recognize him, but Joseph knew who they were. When Joseph told them who he was, they were sorry for all they had done to him. Joseph could have been angry. He could have punished his brothers. Instead, he told them that when they did bad things to him, God used it for good.

Maybe there is someone who is unkind to you. Maybe you know a bully who makes fun of you. Maybe someone has taken something from you. No matter what, God is in control! You can choose to act like Joseph. You can be nice to others even when they aren't nice to you. —T.M.

READ MORE

Not only did Joseph forgive his brothers, he also took care of them when they needed help. Read Genesis 45:9–11 to find out what he did.

FUN FACT

Joseph was only thirty years old when he started ruling over Egypt. He lived for eighty more years, until he was 110!

Let It Show

> Love is patient.
> Love is kind. It does
> not want what
> belongs to others.
> It does not brag.
> It is not proud.
>
> **1 CORINTHIANS 13:4 NIRV**

What is the nicest thing you can say to someone? How about "I love you"?

Parents say "I love you" to their children, and children say it back to their parents. Grandmas and grandpas tell their grandkids "I love you." Aunts and uncles and other relatives may say "I love you." When you love someone, it means you care about them. We can tell people we love them, but we can also show it by the way we act.

Love is more than just words. You can show your love for others by being kind. Do you share your games or books with your friends? That's showing love. Have you helped a brother or sister or parent with chores? That's showing love too!

When you love others, you're happy when good things happen to them. If your friends get a new bike or video game, you can be happy for them. If your brother or sister gets an A on a test, you can say, "Good job!"

When Jesus lived on earth, He showed His love for others in many different ways. He fed people who were hungry. He healed people who were sick. And He died on the cross to take the punishment for our sins.

Love is more than words can say.

It's important to tell others that we love them. But let's be like Jesus and show our love too! —C.B.

FUN FACT

There are different kinds of love: friendship, kinship (or family love), romantic love (between a man and woman), and divine love. Divine love is God's love and is also called agape (uh-GAH-pay) love.

READ MORE

What does 1 Corinthians 13:13 say about love?

Don't Be Afraid

After Moses died, Joshua became the leader of the people of Israel. God told Joshua to take the people into the land that God had promised to them.

But they couldn't just march in and set up camp. First they had to cross the Jordan River—which was flooded. And there was another problem. The people who already lived in the land didn't want to share it. They did not want a million Israelites moving in.

But Joshua trusted God and obeyed Him. He was ready to do whatever God said, and God told Joshua to be strong and brave. God did not want Joshua to be afraid. God promised Joshua that He would go with him wherever he went.

> "Remember that I commanded you to be strong and brave. So don't be afraid. The Lord your God will be with you everywhere you go."
>
> **JOSHUA 1:9 ICB**

God is with me—so I will not be afraid.

So Joshua told the people to get ready to cross the river and enter the land. Then a miracle happened! When the very first people, the priests, stepped into the Jordan River, God stopped the water from flowing. Everyone crossed the river on dry ground! God was with Joshua, just as He had promised.

You can be strong and brave too. You can trust and obey God, just like Joshua did. You may never lead a million people across a flooded river, but there will be things in your life that make you afraid. Talk to God about them, and ask Him to help you. God will be with you just like He was with Joshua. He doesn't want you to be afraid. —C.B.

READ MORE

Did you know Jesus did something important at the Jordan River too? To learn more, read Matthew 3:13–17.

FUN FACT

The Jordan River is about 156 miles (251 kilometers) long.

> "We should remember
> the words that the
> Lord Jesus said,
> 'Giving gifts is more
> satisfying than
> receiving them.'"
>
> **ACTS 20:35 GW**

Be a Giver

Everyone loves getting presents!

Isn't it fun to open a box on your birthday and get a new toy or video game? Have you ever snooped under the Christmas tree to see if any of those beautiful packages are for you? Sometimes you might even get a gift for no special reason. Surprise gifts are especially exciting!

But it can be just as exciting to give a gift. Maybe you made something special for your mom or picked out a brand-new toy for a friend's birthday. It's fun to see the smiles on other people's faces and the joy they get from receiving something you picked out for them.

It's better to give than to receive.

You may have heard someone say, "It's better to give than to receive." Did you know that saying comes from the Bible? Jesus is the one who said it! He was saying that we can be happier when we give things than when we get things. When you give, God uses you to make others happy.

And it's not only presents. You can give to others by speaking a kind word, helping someone out, or sharing food and clothes with people who need them. Giving to others shows your love for Jesus. Giving gifts is really better than receiving them! —T.M.

FUN FACT

The tradition of giving gifts at Christmas began with the wise men who brought gold, frankincense, and myrrh to Jesus.

READ MORE

Read James 1:17.
Where do good gifts come from?

Grapes and Grapevines

> "I am the vine; you are the branches. If you remain in me and I in you, you will bear much fruit; apart from me you can do nothing."
>
> **JOHN 15:5 NIV**

Do you like to eat grapes? Whether they're red or purple or green, grapes are juicy and delicious. They grow on plants called grapevines which grow upward along a fence. The leaves are connected to the vine by branches. The branches connect to the trunk, which connects to the roots underground. All of the parts work together to give the grapes what they need to grow.

Jesus once told His friends that He was a grapevine and they were the branches. As His time on earth grew short, Jesus wanted His disciples to know that His spirit would be with them even after He had gone to heaven. Jesus said that if His disciples stayed connected to Him, like the branches on a grapevine, His power would flow into them and they would grow fruit. But Jesus didn't mean grapes. The fruit He meant was love and joy and peace, and other good things that make people more like Jesus.

I will stay connected to the vine.

When Jesus went to heaven, His disciples continued the work Jesus had started. Because they were connected to Jesus like branches to a grapevine, they became more like Him. They preached about God with boldness and did miracles to help people.

Jesus wants us to stay connected to Him too. How do we do that? By reading the Bible and praying. By loving Jesus and obeying what He tells us to do. When we stay connected to Jesus—the vine—our lives will be "fruitful" for Him! —C.B.

READ MORE

How does Acts 3:1–10 show that Peter and John were becoming more like Jesus?

FUN FACT

China, the United States, Italy, France, and Spain are the countries that grow the most grapes.

Treasure Hunt

> "Again, the kingdom of heaven is like a trader who was looking for fine pearls. He found one that was very valuable. So he went away and sold everything he had. And he bought that pearl."
>
> **MATTHEW 13:45–46 NIRV**

What's the most valuable thing you have? For some people, it's a computer or tablet. Others have an old coin that's been in the family for years. Maybe it's fancy jewelry that used to belong to a grandmother or great-grandmother.

When you have something valuable you take good care of it. You might keep it in a special box or hide it somewhere so no one else can find it. But what if you lost it? That would be upsetting! You would search very hard until you found it. You might even stay up past your bedtime.

In the book of Matthew, Jesus told His disciples that God's kingdom was like a treasure. Jesus told a story about a businessman searching for a pearl—an expensive and precious jewel. When the man found the perfect pearl, he knew it was worth a lot of money. So he sold everything he owned to get money to buy it.

I can search for God's kingdom like it's a treasure.

Jesus came to earth searching for us and gave up all He had to be with us. His love is the most valuable thing we can have. As He helps us understand His love for us, we can show our love for Him. When we give up everything else to put Him first, we're like the man who bought the pearl.

Learning all about Jesus and His kingdom is like hunting for treasure. If we spend time searching, we will find something priceless. —T.M.

FUN FACT

The largest pearl ever discovered weighs over fourteen pounds (six kilograms) and is worth millions of dollars!

READ MORE

Read Proverbs 2:1–5.
What else should we search for like a treasure?

Important Advice

There's an old familiar saying that goes like this: "If at first you don't succeed, try, try again."

What does it mean to "succeed"? To succeed, or to find "success," is to have things turn out the way you want them to. Success for many people is being popular or having lots of money and things. But real success comes from obeying God and doing what He wants you to do.

King David ruled God's people, the Israelites, for forty years. When he was old and about to die, David gave his son Solomon some important advice. David told Solomon to obey God and follow His commands. He said that if Solomon wanted to be successful, he needed to do everything that God expected him to do.

David's advice is for us too! To be successful, we need to trust and obey God. He will guide us and help us to do what He wants us to do. Remember that success isn't just having a lot of money or being popular. Success means loving God and caring for other people.

Do you want to be successful? Then listen to the important advice of King David: "Do everything the LORD your God requires." —C.B.

> "Do everything the LORD your God requires. Live the way he wants you to. Obey his orders and commands. Keep his laws and rules. Do everything that is written in the Law of Moses. Then you will have success in everything you do. You will succeed everywhere you go."
>
> **1 KINGS 2:3 NIRV**

Success comes from obeying God.

READ MORE
**Look up 2 Chronicles 9:22.
What does it say about King Solomon?**

Follow the Leader

Have you ever played the game "Follow the Leader"? When you're the leader, everyone else has to do whatever you do. If you jump on one foot, all the others have to jump on one foot. If you sing a silly song, everyone else sings it too. When another person becomes the leader, you have to copy whatever she does.

Kids (and grown-ups too) often copy the things their friends do—even when they're not playing a game. That's why it's so important to choose good friends. When we "follow the leader," we want to be like friends who love God and do what's right. We are wise when we choose friends who know it's right to obey parents and respect teachers. We become better people when we play with friends who are kind to others and share and take turns. But following someone who often gets into trouble might get us into trouble too.

When Jesus was living on earth, He invited some men to follow Him. They are known as Jesus' "twelve disciples." Many of them became His good friends as they followed Jesus and did the things He told them to do.

Jesus still asks people to follow Him today. How can we do that? By learning more about Him from the Bible. God's Word tells us how Jesus wants us to live and what He wants us to do. You'll never follow a better leader than Jesus! —C.B.

I will choose to follow good friends.

FUN FACT

Sheep "follow the leader." They follow the sheep that is in front of them. If the lead sheep goes somewhere it shouldn't, the rest of the flock often go there too!

READ MORE

Read Matthew 4:18–22 to learn about the first four disciples who followed Jesus. What were their names?

A Brave Choice

Do you know someone who is brave? Is it your dad because he catches the spiders in your house? Is it an older brother or sister who isn't afraid of the dark? Kids often think the biggest and strongest people seem the bravest. It can be hard to be brave when you are young. But with God on your side, you can choose to be brave even when you're afraid.

> "What if you don't say anything at this time? . . . It's possible that you became queen for a time just like this."
> **ESTHER 4:14 NIRV**

Esther was a beautiful young woman who lived in Old Testament times. She was brought to the king of Persia's palace for a beauty contest to decide who would be the next queen. Out of all the girls in the contest, Esther won! Everyone in the palace loved her. But Esther had a secret that no one else in the palace knew. She was Jewish.

With God on my side, I can be brave.

One of the king's top officials hated the Jewish people and wanted the king to kill them. So Esther had a tough choice to make. Her cousin Mordecai told her to talk to the king. But Esther knew if she went to the king without permission, she could be killed. Mordecai told her it was the right thing to do, and Esther decided to do it. When Esther went to see the king, he was pleased. He listened to her and agreed to save the Jewish people!

Esther's story shows how God uses people for His special plans. God gave Esther the courage to do what He wanted her to do. And He will give you courage when you need it too. —T.M.

READ MORE

Read Daniel 3 to learn about three other people who made a brave choice.

FUN FACT

Esther and the other girls in the beauty contest went through a whole year of beauty treatments! (See Esther 2:12.)

Do-over

Anyone who
believes in Christ
is a new creation.
The old is gone!
The new has come!

2 CORINTHIANS 5:17 NIRV

Have you ever been given a do-over when you messed up? Maybe you got a bad grade on a test and your teacher let you retake it. Maybe you kicked the ball the wrong way and your coach let you try again. Do-overs are great! It's nice to be able to start over when something doesn't go right the first time.

People who believe in Jesus get a great big do-over. God's Word tells us that anyone who believes that Jesus is the Son of God is a "new creation." That means the bad

Christians are a new creation.

choices they made before they trusted Jesus are not held against them. Their sins have all been forgiven. They can now live a life that pleases God.

When God looks at people who believe in Jesus, He doesn't see their mess-ups and sins. He sees Jesus! Do you know what that means? Because Jesus never, ever sinned, God sees His perfection instead of what we have done wrong.

Even after we've become Christians, we sometimes still mess up. But when we do, God gives us more do-overs. When we're sorry for our sins and ask God to forgive us, Jesus wipes those sins away. He's just like a teacher erasing words from the board at school. Now that's a great do-over! —T.M.

READ MORE

What does God tell us in Isaiah 43:18–19?

FUN FACT

A do-over
in the game of golf
is called a mulligan.

Keep Good Company

> Godly people are careful about the friends they choose. But the way of sinners leads them down the wrong path.
>
> **PROVERBS 12:26 NIRV**

Do you know what it means to "keep good company"? It means to spend time with the right kind of people. Having the right kind of friends is important.

Abram was a man who obeyed God. He had a nephew named Lot. One day they decided it was time to move away from each other. They needed more space for their animals and families. Lot made a bad choice. He moved close to the cities of Sodom and Gomorrah. The people who lived in those cities did not obey God. Lot moved even closer until he was living right inside Sodom. He did not keep good company.

Before long, Lot was in trouble. The kings of Sodom and Gomorrah got into a big fight with seven other kings. During the battle, Lot and his family were kidnapped!

It's important to choose good friends.

When Abram heard about it, he built an army of more than three hundred men. The army divided up into groups and made a surprise attack. Abram was able to bring back everything the enemy had stolen, including Lot.

You might think that Lot would have learned a lesson. But he went back to live in the city of Sodom, where the people were still disobeying God. And one day, Lot lost everything he had.

Always choose good friends, and be sure to keep good company! —C.B.

FUN FACT

A famous poet in Greece more than two thousand years ago said, "Every man is known by the company he keeps."

READ MORE

Read Genesis 14:22–24.
Why did Abram decide not to keep anything from Sodom?

Bird Watching

> "Aren't two sparrows sold for only a penny? But not one of them falls to the ground without your Father knowing it. He even counts every hair on your head! So don't be afraid. You are worth more than many sparrows."
>
> MATTHEW 10:29–31 NIRV

You've probably seen sparrows. They are small brown birds that like to live near people. Sparrows are one of the most common birds in the world, found in Africa, Europe, North and South America, and parts of Asia. Because they're so common, sparrows don't get a lot of attention. Even in Bible times, they were not worth very much.

One time, Jesus told His disciples not to be afraid of the people who were against them. Jesus knew that some people might treat His disciples badly. But He reminded them that God is always watching over them and always caring for them. He told His disciples that God watches over and cares for the sparrows. If He does that, God will certainly watch over and care for His people.

God watches the sparrows—and He watches me.

God loves sparrows because He created them. He helps them find food to eat and places to rest. He knows if even one of those little birds falls to the ground. And do you know what? God loves you the same way! He created you. He gives you food to eat, clothes to wear, and a place to live. He even knows how many hairs you have on your head.

That's why Jesus tells us, "Don't be afraid." God cares about little brown sparrows, and you are worth much, much more than sparrows. —C.B.

READ MORE

Jesus talked about birds another time.
Read Matthew 6:25–27. What did He say?

FUN FACT

House sparrows are almost everywhere—from high up on New York City's Empire State Building to deep in a mine in Yorkshire, England.

Old Enough

Don't let anyone look down on you for being young. Instead, make your speech, behavior, love, faith, and purity an example for other believers.

1 TIMOTHY 4:12 GW

Has anyone ever told you, "You're not old enough to do that"? When you're young, it can feel like you're not allowed to do many things. You have to be a certain height to ride a roller coaster. You can't stay up as late as your mom or dad. You can't ride your bike too far away from home.

You might even feel like people don't listen to what you say because you're young. When that happens, you may want to grow up quickly so people will respect you more.

The Bible tells us about a young man named Timothy. He studied God's teachings under the apostle Paul and went on missionary trips with him. Timothy loved God. Even though he was young, he was grown-up in his faith. Timothy became a pastor in the city of Ephesus. Paul wrote a letter telling Timothy to stay strong in his faith and be a good example, even though he was young.

You can be a good example too—even to people older than you. The way you act can show others that you love God. When you say please and thank you, others will see you're respectful. When you help clean up a neighbor's yard, people will see that you serve others. When you pray before a meal or read a Bible verse out loud, others will see that you want to be close to God. Even young children can show others that God is great! —T.M.

I can be a good example, no matter how old I am.

FUN FACT

Joshua Williams started an organization called Joshua's Heart to help hungry people in his community. Joshua began this project when he was only five years old!

READ MORE

Read John 13:13–17 in your Bible.
How does Jesus set an example for us?

Keep the Lights On

It's hard to see in the dark. If you're in a dark room, you want to switch on the lights. If you're outdoors at night, you want to carry a flashlight. If a storm knocks out power to your house, you want to have candles or a lantern to be able to see.

> This is the message we heard from Christ and are reporting to you: God is light, and there isn't any darkness in him.
>
> **1 JOHN 1:5 GW**

Being in the dark can be dangerous. If you can't see, it's easy to trip and fall or bump into things. And can you imagine what it would be like if cars didn't have headlights? Drivers couldn't see where they were going and might crash into other cars or trees or buildings.

God is light.

Sin is a kind of darkness. When we choose to do wrong, it's like bringing darkness into our lives. It's a dangerous way to live and bad things can happen.

But the Bible tells us that God is light. When we believe in God and learn how He wants us to live, it's like turning all the lights on. God helps us to see what is right and wrong. He helps us to see how much He loves us and cares for us. He helps us to see all the things that can hurt us.

With God there is no darkness. God not only gives us light, He is the light. And God's light never goes out!
—C.B.

FUN FACT

Because of the way the earth is tilted, people who live near the Arctic Circle may not see the sun for many days or weeks. At other times of the year it may be light for a very long time.

READ MORE

Read Genesis 1:14–19 to learn about the lights God created. Why did He create these lights?

> Simon answered, "Master, we've worked hard all night and haven't caught anything. But because you say so, I will let down the nets."
>
> **LUKE 5:5 NIV**

Because You Say So

One night Jesus' disciples were out fishing. But they didn't catch anything. So they rowed back to shore and began washing their nets. Jesus came along and talked to Simon Peter, one of His disciples. Jesus told Simon Peter to row back into the deep water and drop his nets again. Simon Peter was probably very tired. He had fished all night without catching anything. He didn't feel like going back out with the nets he had just cleaned. But Peter obeyed, because Jesus said so.

Do you know what happened next? The disciples caught so many fish that their nets began to break! They had to shout for their friends to help them drag all the fish to shore!

The disciples were amazed. They knew Jesus had performed a miracle. Then Jesus told them they would start fishing for men. Just like the disciples had caught a lot of fish, Jesus wanted them to bring many people to Him to become His followers.

Jesus knows best.

This story shows us what trust in Jesus looks like. Simon Peter did something just because Jesus said so. Jesus responded to that trust by performing a miracle and giving Simon Peter a new job: fishing for people!

You can trust Jesus like that too. You can invite your friends to church or pray with them or share your things with them, just because Jesus says so. When you trust Him, He will respond to your trust. —C.B.

FUN FACT

Early Christians used a fish picture to stand for their faith. Those Christians spoke the Greek language. When they took the first letters of the words for "Jesus Christ, Son of God, Savior," they spelled the Greek word for "fish": ΙΧΘΥΣ.

READ MORE

Before Jesus went back to heaven, He said other things about bringing people to Him. Read Mark 16:15–20 to see what He said.

A Shepherd's Love

A shepherd is *someone who takes care of sheep. Depending on where you live, you might never see a shepherd working in a field. But when the Bible was being written, shepherds were very common. Because people in ancient Israel knew shepherds well, the Bible writers often used shepherds as an example of God's love.*

The LORD is my shepherd. I am never in need.
PSALM 23:1 GW

Shepherds' duties include keeping their flock together, guiding the sheep where they need to go, and protecting the sheep from other animals that could hurt them. King David, who was also a shepherd, wrote Psalm 23, one of the best-known psalms in the Bible. It explains how God is our shepherd.

Just like a shepherd takes care of his sheep, God takes care of us. Shepherds lead their sheep to green fields when they need to lie down to rest. God gives us times of rest and sleep when we're tired. A shepherd uses his voice or a special stick to guide the sheep where they need to go. God guides us and speaks to us through the Bible. When sheep travel through a dangerous area where they might be attacked, the shepherd is there to protect them. God does the same for us—He is right beside us when we face scary things, and He protects us from harm.

Sheep need a lot of help. So do we! God promises to meet all of our needs, just like a shepherd takes care of his sheep. —T.M.

The Lord is my shepherd.

READ MORE
What does the prophet Isaiah say about Jesus in Isaiah 40:11?

FUN FACT
The wooden stick a shepherd carries is called a staff. It can be used to guide the sheep on the path or to fight off animals that attack the sheep.

Jesus and Zacchaeus

When Jesus was passing through the city of Jericho, many people rushed to see Him. Zacchaeus wanted to see Jesus too, but he was a short man. Poor Zacchaeus couldn't get a glimpse of Jesus above all the people standing around him!

That's when Zacchaeus got an idea. He ran ahead of the crowd and climbed up into a sycamore tree. Zacchaeus knew he would be high enough above the crowd to see Jesus as He passed by. But Zacchaeus didn't expect what happened next.

When Jesus came near the tree, He looked up and said, "Zacchaeus, come down! I must stay at your house today." Zacchaeus was excited! He quickly climbed down the tree and welcomed Jesus to his home.

Some people weren't happy about Jesus visiting Zacchaeus's house. Zacchaeus was a tax collector—his job was to take money from people in the town. And he wasn't always honest when he asked for their money. Sometimes Zacchaeus cheated the people. That's why they didn't like him. They were surprised that Jesus would spend time with a dishonest man.

Jesus helps people change from the inside out.

But Jesus didn't judge Zacchaeus the way others did. Jesus knew Zacchaeus could change. After spending time with Jesus, Zacchaeus realized that he had been treating other people badly. He told Jesus he would pay back everyone he cheated. Zacchaeus became a generous person.

Jesus knows people can change. He's not looking for perfect people. All Jesus asks is that we believe in Him and love Him. Then others will see the change in our lives. —T.M.

FUN FACT

The type of tree that Zacchaeus climbed can reach a height of about fifty feet (fifteen meters). It grows a kind of fruit called figs.

READ MORE

Read Acts 9:1–18 to find out about another man who changed from the inside out.

Don't Give Up

"I'm bored!" How many times have you said that? It's easy to get bored after you've done the same thing for a while. Did you ever get a toy or video game that looked really fun? When you first get something new, it's really exciting. But after a while it doesn't seem so interesting. It's normal to get tired of doing the same thing over and over—even if it's something we like.

> So let's not get tired of doing what is good. At just the right time we will reap a harvest of blessing if we don't give up.
>
> **GALATIANS 6:9 NLT**

The Bible tells us we should never get tired of doing good things. The apostle Paul, who wrote the book of Galatians, seemed to understand that people can get bored doing the same things over and over. That's why he told us not to give up. When it comes to helping others and doing good, it's important that we don't get bored or quit before we're finished.

I won't get tired of doing what is good.

Continuing to do good things and choosing to follow God's rules isn't always easy. Sometimes your friends might not understand why you serve God. At other times you may not feel like doing the right thing. But God uses people who love Him to accomplish His plans for the world. Continue to do good things and don't give up, because God is worthy of it. And He promises to bless those who obey and serve Him! —T.M.

FUN FACT

Mother Teresa, famous for caring for the poor and sick of India, started doing good for others in 1948. Her first year was very hard and she almost gave up. By the time she died in 1997, her work had spread to more than one hundred countries!

READ MORE

What does 1 Corinthians 15:58 tell us about doing God's work?

As long as Moses held
his hands up, the
Israelites would
win the fight.
EXODUS 17:11 ICB

Helping Hands

After the Israelites left Egypt, they lived in a desert for many years. One day they were attacked by people called the Amalekites. Moses told Joshua to choose men to fight against the Amalekites. While Joshua and his men went out to fight, Moses went to stand on top of a hill to watch.

Moses took his brother, Aaron, and a man named Hur with him. Moses held up his hands, and the Israelites started to win the battle. But whenever he lowered his hands, the Amalekites would begin to win. After a while, Moses' arms got tired. So Aaron and Hur found a rock for Moses to sit on, then each man held up Moses' hands until the Israelites won the fight. After the battle, Moses built an altar to God. He named it "The Lord Is My Banner." Moses said, "I lifted my hands toward the Lord's throne."

I will reach out to God for help.

Moses lifted his hands to God because he knew his help came from God. And when Moses got tired, his friends were there to lift him up. Just like Moses, we can raise our hands to God for help. But we can also bow our knees to pray. There is no wrong way to ask God for help! Whether we sit or stand or kneel or lie down, God wants us to come to Him for help. He hears our prayers. He is strong and mighty. Reach out to Him! —C.B.

FUN FACT
In many churches, the service ends with a blessing called a benediction. The pastor reads a blessing such as Numbers 6:22–27 as he raises his hands to God.

READ MORE
Lamentations 3:41 tells us something else we can lift to the Lord. What is it?

Vocabulary Words

Do you get lists of vocabulary words at school? You have to learn how to spell the words as well as learn what the words mean. And you'll probably have to take a test on them at some point!

Learning vocabulary words helps us to understand what we read. And what we read helps us understand the world around us. Grace, mercy, and peace are three words that are found in the Bible. They can be your vocabulary words for today.

> Grace, mercy, and peace, which come from God the Father and from Jesus Christ—the Son of the Father—will continue to be with us who live in truth and love.
>
> 2 JOHN 3 NLT

Grace is help and love God gives us even though we don't deserve it. It's like a teacher giving you an A on a test after you got all the answers wrong. None of us are perfect, but God loves us anyway. He gives us many blessings that we do not deserve. When we believe in Jesus and turn away from the wrong things we do, we are saved by God's grace.

Grace, mercy, and peace are gifts of God's love.

Mercy is God's gentle forgiveness. If you disobey your parents and they decide not to punish you—that's mercy. Because of God's mercy we are not punished for our sins. We deserve to be punished, but Jesus took that punishment for us when He died on the cross.

Peace is a calm feeling we have inside because we know God loves us and will care for us no matter what. Peace is the opposite of worry. When things in life don't go well for us, we can still have peace by trusting in God.

Grace, mercy, and peace are all gifts from God. They're also good vocabulary words! —C.B.

READ MORE

Read Ephesians 2:4–8.
What do these verses tell us about God's grace and mercy?

FUN FACT

Most three-year-old kids have a vocabulary of about two hundred words. By age five, they know up to two thousand words!

Confusion in the City

So the Lord caused them to spread out from there all over the whole world.
GENESIS 11:9 ICB

Do you remember the flood God sent in Noah's time? After the flood, Noah's sons had many children. Their families grew and grew. God told all those people to go to different parts of the earth. But the people didn't want to live in different places. They didn't listen to God.

At that time everyone spoke one language. They said to each other, "Let's make some bricks. Let's build a city with a tower that reaches into the sky. We will become famous and we won't become scattered all over the earth."

So they made their bricks and began to build their fancy tower. When God saw what the people were doing, He decided to stop it. God confused the people's language so they could no longer work together. When the people realized they were speaking different languages, they stopped building the tower. They spread out across the land the way God wanted them to. The place where the people tried to build the tower was called Babel.

These people learned that God was much stronger than they were. When God wants something to happen, it will happen. God wants His people to obey Him—but when they don't obey, He will still do what He knows is best.

No matter what people do, God will always have His way.

Today there are many people who are famous, smart, or important. Some people act as if they don't need God. But that's not true. Everyone needs God, and no one will ever be greater than He is. —C.B.

FUN FACT

There are close to seven thousand languages in the world. The complete Bible has been translated into about five hundred languages, and the New Testament has been translated into nearly thirteen hundred languages.

READ MORE
What does Isaiah 55:10–11 tell us about the words that God speaks?

One Way

We often need directions to find our way to a new place. We might use a map. We might use the Internet or a GPS unit, or we might even ask another person. If you asked a friend how to get to his house, you'd want him to give you the clearest directions possible. If he said, "Well you can take Third Street and then turn right on Maple Avenue, or you can take Tenth Street and then turn left on Fourth, or if you want to go another way, you can go down Main Street and then turn left on Meadow Street," that would be confusing and frustrating! If you want to get somewhere, you need clear directions!

> Jesus told him, "I am the way, the truth, and the life. No one can come to the Father except through me."
>
> JOHN 14:6 NLT

One day Jesus told His disciples that He was making a place for them in heaven. Thomas asked, "How can we know the way?" Jesus didn't give a bunch of different answers. He told Thomas the only way to heaven is through believing in Him. "I am the way!" Jesus said.

Jesus is the way to heaven.

When we believe that Jesus died to save us from our sins—when we ask Him to be our Savior—we will go to heaven when we die. Jesus is the way to God the Father. You don't need to find another way, because Jesus is the only way. If your friends ask you how to get to heaven, you can give them good directions. You can say, "Believe in Jesus as your Savior. He is the way!" —C.B.

FUN FACT

GPS stands for "Global Positioning System." It uses twenty-four satellites, floating in space above the earth, to help people find their way. GPS was first used by the military but is now available for anyone to use.

READ MORE

While they were in prison, Paul and Silas gave directions to someone. Read Acts 16:23–34 to find out what happened.

> Dear friends, let us continue to love one another, for love comes from God. Anyone who loves is a child of God and knows God.
>
> 1 JOHN 4:7 NLT

Love Is from God

Have you ever given a valentine to a friend or to someone in your family? On Valentine's Day many people give cards or flowers or candy to show their love. The Bible says that love comes from God. If we are God's children, we need to love others the way that God loves them.

Jesus talked a lot about loving our neighbors. But He didn't mean only the people who live on our street. One time Jesus told a story to help people understand who their neighbors really are. Jesus said, "A man was traveling down a road when some robbers attacked him. They tore his clothes, beat him up, and left him on the side of the road. Another man came along and saw the hurt man, but didn't stop to help him. Then another man walked by and didn't stop to help him either. A third man came by and stopped to help the man who was hurt. He put the man on his donkey and brought him to an inn. He paid the innkeeper to take care of the man, and even offered to give the innkeeper more money if he needed it."

I will show love the way God wants me to.

Then Jesus asked which of the three men in the story showed love to the man who was hurt. The people knew the answer—it was the third man, who stopped to help the person who was hurt. Jesus said, "That's right. Now go and do the same thing."

Valentine's Day is fun, but showing love to others is better than any valentine card!
—C.B.

FUN FACT

Around the world, approximately one billion Valentine cards are sent each year.

READ MORE

What does 1 Corinthians 13:1–7 tell us about love?

A Faithful Woman

"Rahab and all those
who are with her in
her house must
be spared. That's
because she hid the
spies we sent."
JOSHUA 6:17 NIRV

God told the Israelites to take over the city of Jericho. He wanted His people to live there. Israel's leader, Joshua, told the Israelites to destroy everything in the city as an offering to God.

Before the Israelites attacked Jericho, they sent two spies into the city. While they were in Jericho, the spies stayed at the house of a woman named Rahab. The king of Jericho heard there were spies from Israel searching his city. He wanted to capture them. But Rahab hid the spies from the king when his men came looking for them.

Rahab had heard stories about God's miracles. She knew how God had helped the Israelites escape from Egypt. Rahab could see that God was on the side of the Israelites and that He had helped them defeat many enemies. She believed that the God of the Israelites was the true God of the universe.

We are saved by faith.

Rahab asked the spies to protect her when the Israelites took over Jericho. The spies told her to hang a red rope out her window as a sign to the soldiers. When they saw the rope, they would save Rahab and her whole family.

On the day the Israelites attacked Jericho, Rahab and her family were the only people who were saved. Because of Rahab's faith, God saved her and blessed her. She became the great-great grandmother of King David—which means she was a relative of Jesus!

Rahab did not live in a city where the people believed in God. But because she had faith in the one true God, she was saved. —T.M.

READ MORE
Read Ephesians 2:8–9.
Where does salvation come from?

FUN FACT
Jericho is known as "the city of palm trees." It has many streams of water, which is why people have wanted to live there for thousands of years.

Praise the Lord for the glory of his name. Bring your offering to him. Worship the Lord because he is holy.

1 CHRONICLES 16:29 ICB

Praise the Lord!

When David was king of Israel, he wanted the people to praise God with instruments and songs. He chose a man named Asaph to be the worship leader. Asaph played the cymbals while others played harps and lyres. There were also two priests who blew trumpets. Asaph and his team had the job of singing praises to God.

In our churches today, there are people like Asaph. They have the responsibility to lead others in praise and worship. When we sing songs of praise to God, it shows that we love Him. Singing praises is one way we worship God. Our songs can help us remember how great and holy God is. They might remind us of how much God loves us—and how much we love Him. Singing songs of praise to God can help us feel close to Him.

I can praise God anytime and anywhere.

God loves to hear your songs of praise. It doesn't matter if you're a good singer or not. You can sing to God anywhere—you don't have to be in church to praise Him. You can sing songs you learned at church, or make up your own. Our songs of praise please God! So sing out loud and let God hear your praises! —C.B.

FUN FACT

A lyre is a stringed musical instrument that was used in ancient Greece. The sound box was usually made from a turtle shell. The lyre was often used to provide music for singing.

READ MORE

Psalm 150 tells us how to praise the Lord with music.
How many different instruments are
mentioned in this Psalm?

Two Builders

Everyone likes to hear a good story! Stories are fun to listen to—and sometimes they teach us a good lesson.

When Jesus taught the people who followed Him, He often told stories. His stories are called parables. Jesus told parables to help people understand more about God. Some people understood the parables, but others didn't.

One day Jesus told the story of two men who built their houses on different foundations. A foundation is the base or bottom part of a house that holds up the rest of the house.

In Jesus' parable, a wise man built his house on rock. It was a solid foundation. When the rain came down, the wind blew hard, and the water rose, the house stood firm. But a foolish man built his house on sand. Sand is not a good foundation and will not support a house for very long. When the rain came down, the wind blew hard, and the water rose, the foolish man's house tumbled down!

Jesus said that anyone who listens to His teaching and does what He says is like the wise man who built his house on a rock. Like the person who builds a house on a solid foundation, we can build our lives on Jesus. When trouble comes, we will be strong.

Since you're young, this is a perfect time to build your life on a solid foundation. Jesus is the rock! —C.B.

> "Anyone who listens to my teaching and follows it is wise, like a person who builds a house on solid rock."
>
> MATTHEW 7:24 NLT

Jesus is my foundation.

READ MORE
What does Psalm 18:1–2 tell us about God?

FUN FACT

The world's largest tree house is located in Crossville, Tennessee. It is ten thousand square feet in size—almost four times larger than most American homes!

Call on Jesus

Because Jesus experienced temptation when he suffered, he is able to help others when they are tempted.

HEBREWS 2:18 GW

Have you ever wanted to keep something that wasn't yours? Imagine finding a brand-new ball on the playground. Though you know it belongs to someone else, you still want to keep it. When we want to do something we know is wrong, it's called temptation.

Some people are tempted to lie or steal. Kids can be tempted to cheat on a test at school. You can even be tempted to say something mean to another person.

The very first people God made were tempted. Adam and Eve lived in the Garden of Eden. God told them they could eat the fruit from any tree in the garden, except for one. When they were tempted to disobey God, they gave in to that temptation. They sinned against God and brought much trouble into the world.

Did you know that Jesus was tempted too? But Jesus never gave in to temptation. He knew what was right, and He always chose to do the right thing. But Jesus understands how hard it is when we face temptation. He wants to help us be strong and do the right thing.

It is not a sin to be tempted. But it is a sin to do the wrong thing after we are tempted. When we are tempted to do wrong, we can call out to Jesus for help. And we can ask God to keep us from being tempted. God will help us to live the right way.

And if you ever find a brand-new ball on the playground, you can take it to the lost and found. —C.B.

When I am tempted, I will call on Jesus.

FUN FACT

France was home of the first lost-and-found office in 1805. The emperor Napoleon told police to start the office as a place to collect things found on the streets of Paris.

READ MORE

Do you know how Jesus handled temptation?
Read Matthew 4:1–11 to find out what Jesus did.

Contest on a Mountain

Elijah was a prophet who served the one true God. One day God sent Elijah to see Ahab, an evil king who ruled the people of Israel. King Ahab had turned the people away from God, and they began worshipping a false god.

Elijah told King Ahab to send the leaders of the false religion to the top of a hill called Mount Carmel. Then Elijah challenged King Ahab and his men to a contest. It was Elijah all by himself against 450 leaders on the other side. Elijah told them to build an altar. He told them to ask their god to send fire to their altar.

The 450 men prayed and cried out to their god all day long. But nothing happened. There was no fire, not even a spark. Then Elijah told all the people to come over to his side. As the people watched, Elijah rebuilt the altar of the Lord that had been torn down. He asked men to pour four big jars of water over the altar. Then he told them to do it again. And then he told them to do it a third time!

> "O LORD, God of Abraham, Isaac, and Jacob, prove today that you are God in Israel and that I am your servant. Prove that I have done all this at your command."
>
> **1 KINGS 18:36 NLT**

I will worship the one true God.

When everything was ready, Elijah asked God to show that He was the real God. Elijah asked God to change the people's hearts. And God heard Elijah's prayer. He sent fire from heaven that burned up the altar and even the water around it! When the people saw that, they shouted, "The Lord is God! The Lord is God!"

Elijah believed in God's power, and we can too. Even when others don't understand our faith, we know that we worship the one true God. —T.M.

READ MORE

Read James 5:17–18.
What else did Elijah ask God to do to show His power?

FUN FACT

The altars the Israelites built to God were usually made from one of three materials: dirt, stone, or a yellowish-brown metal called bronze.

> He who watches over
> you won't get tired . . .
> or go to sleep.
>
> PSALM 121:3–4 NIRV

Up All Night

Have you ever stayed up late? Maybe your mom or dad let you stay up until midnight on New Year's Eve. Or maybe you had a friend spend the night, and you told stories and giggled way past your bedtime. But no matter how late you stayed up, eventually you did go to sleep.

We all have to sleep at some point. We can't skip our sleep because our bodies need rest. Sleep helps us to have strength and energy for the next day.

It isn't like that with God, though. The Bible tells us that God never sleeps. He never even gets tired! It's hard to imagine having never-ending strength and energy—but God does. That's another example of His greatness. Every second of the day and night, God is watching over all His creation. He's always taking care of everything. And that includes you.

Did you ever wake up at night and notice your parents were still awake? Somehow, the house feels safer when you know someone is still up. But even after your parents go to sleep, you can still feel that safe because God stays up all night watching over you. Daytime or nighttime, God is awake—and He is taking care of you. —T.M.

God is always watching over me.

FUN FACT

In 1964, a seventeen-year-old named Randy Gardner stayed awake for eleven days and twenty-four minutes. Many believe that's a world record!

READ MORE

Read Exodus 12:31–42 to learn about an important event that happened during the night.

Time Stands Still

The king of Jerusalem was afraid. He heard that Joshua and the Israelites had taken over Jericho and defeated a city called Ai. Both of these cities were large and strong.

The Israelites had made peace with an important city called Gibeon. Because Gibeon was on Israel's side, the king of Jerusalem was even more scared. He knew if the Israelites and Gibeon worked together, they could take over his kingdom. So he called together other kings from around Jerusalem. They agreed to attack Gibeon and take it over. That way they would all be protected from the Israelites.

The people of Gibeon sent a message to Joshua asking for help. They wanted Joshua to come and fight for them. God said He would be with Joshua and help him defeat the evil kings. So Joshua and his army marched all night to Gibeon. At daylight, they began to fight. God made the Israelites strong in this battle and helped them win. God also dropped big hailstones on the enemy armies.

> So the sun stood still. The moon stopped. They didn't move again until the nation won the battle over its enemies. . . . The sun stopped in the middle of the sky. It didn't go down for about a full day. There has never been a day like it before or since.
>
> **JOSHUA 10:13–14 NIRV**

God can do great things for His people.

As the day went on, Joshua prayed an amazing prayer. "Sun, stop over Gibeon," he said. "Moon, stand still over the Valley of Aijalon." God listened to Joshua's prayer! He held the sun in place for almost a whole day so Israel could finish the fight. God fought for His people and gave them victory!

Nothing is too hard for God. He is faithful to those who trust Him. If God can stop the sun and the moon in the sky, He can help you with your problems too. —T.M.

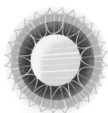

🕮 **READ MORE**

Read 2 Kings 20:8–11.
What did Isaiah ask God to do? Did God do it?

FUN FACT

A solar eclipse happens when the moon moves between the sun and earth. During a solar eclipse, the earth is in the moon's shadow.

A joyful heart
makes a
cheerful face.

PROVERBS 15:13 GW

From the Inside Out

Have you ever heard someone say, "It's what's on the inside that counts"? That means it doesn't matter what you look like. The most important part of a person is what's in her heart.

The way we treat people shows what we're like on the inside. The words we say let others know who we really are. If there's joy in your heart, it will show in the way you live your life.

God is the one who gives us joy. When you love God, He puts joy in your heart. With God's joy inside you, you can have peace even when things aren't going the way you'd like them to. When you have joy in your heart, it's hard to keep it inside. It will bubble out of you like fizz from a bottle of soda!

Joy in your heart puts a grin on your face. You can smile at the people you pass on the sidewalk. You can encourage a friend who is having a bad day. Sharing your joy with others is a great way to show God's love.

Just like it's tough to smile when you feel sad, it's hard to feel hopeless when you have God's joy and peace in your heart. God wants that joy and peace to be on display to everyone around you. So let it flow from the inside out! —T.M.

God puts joy in my heart.

FUN FACT

Some people believe kids smile much more than adults. Kids smile as many as four hundred times a day. That's a lot of joy you can share with your friends and family!

READ MORE
What does Proverbs 17:22 say about being cheerful?

God is able to do
far more than we
could ever ask for
or imagine. He does
everything by his
power that is
working in us.

EPHESIANS 3:20 NIRV

Keep Pouring

Elisha was a prophet of God who continued the work of Elijah. One day a poor widow came to Elisha for help. She had two sons to care for, and all she owned was a little olive oil. When that was gone, she would have nothing.

Elisha told the woman to ask her neighbors for empty jars. He told her to get as many as she could, then start pouring her oil into the empty jars. The widow didn't ask questions. She trusted Elisha and did what he told her to do.

When the widow filled a jar with oil, her sons would bring her another jar to fill. She poured and poured and poured until every jar was full! When she filled the last jar, the oil from her own jar stopped flowing. With all the oil she now had, she could sell the jars and have enough money to take care of her sons.

God can do more than I can imagine.

This is one of many amazing stories that we read in the Bible. It's another example of how God can do impossible things. The Bible doesn't tell us how many empty jars the widow brought to her house. Do you think if she had borrowed even more jars, that those jars would have been filled too?

God can do much more than we can imagine. When we trust and obey God, His blessings pour over us like oil that doesn't stop. —C.B.

READ MORE

1 Kings 17:1–16 tells us a story about a widow who fed the prophet Elijah. Read the story to find out about another miracle.

FUN FACT

Olive oil is made by squeezing olives. Almost all of the olive oil in the world comes from countries around the Mediterranean Sea.

> For this reason we must pay closer attention to what we have heard. Then we won't drift away from the truth.
>
> **HEBREWS 2:1 GW**

Drop Anchor

Have you ever seen a big, heavy anchor on the side of a ship? Anchors are made of metal and sink fast to the ocean floor when they're thrown over the side of a boat. Do you know what an anchor is used for? If a ship's captain wants to keep the boat in a certain place, he drops the anchor on a long chain into the water. The anchor digs into the sand on the ocean floor and keeps the boat from drifting. When the waves start rolling and the wind starts blowing, the boat stays where it should.

The Bible is like an anchor in our lives. It shows us the teachings of Jesus and helps us to know how we should live. When we obey Jesus' words and do what He says, it's like throwing an anchor over the side of a boat. It holds us right where we need to be. It keeps us from being pushed and pulled in the wrong direction.

Jesus is my anchor.

There may be times when other people want you to do something you know is wrong. Sometimes you might want to hide when others make fun of your beliefs. But if we stay anchored to Jesus and do what He tells us to do, we'll be right where He wants us. We won't drift away. —T.M.

FUN FACT

Some boats use a "mushroom anchor." It was given this name because it's shaped like an upside-down mushroom. This kind of anchor is used where the ocean bottom is very soft.

READ MORE

What does Hebrews 6:18–19 say about anchors?

Walking on Water

Peter and the other disciples had had a long day. Crowds of people followed the disciples as they traveled with Jesus. Jesus spent the day teaching and even performed a miracle to feed five thousand people who were listening on a mountainside. When the long day was over, Jesus sent the disciples ahead of Him on a boat to cross the Sea of Galilee.

As the disciples sailed into the night, the wind started to blow and waves crashed against the boat. Suddenly, the disciples saw someone walking on the water toward them! They thought they were seeing a ghost—and they were afraid. But Jesus called out, "Don't be afraid. I am here."

Peter said, "Lord, if it's really you, tell me to come to you walking on the water." Jesus told Peter to come, so Peter got out of the boat. He placed his feet on the water.

> So Peter went over the side of the boat and walked on the water toward Jesus. But when he saw the strong wind and the waves, he was terrified and began to sink. "Save me, Lord!" he shouted.
>
> MATTHEW 14:29–30 NLT

I can keep my thoughts fixed on Jesus.

He took a step. Then he took another. Peter was walking on the water to Jesus! But then Peter noticed the strong wind and the big waves. He took his eyes off of Jesus—and he quickly began to sink. Peter cried out to Jesus for help, and Jesus reached out His hand to save Peter.

Sometimes, like Peter, we think about things around us instead of thinking about Jesus. When we take our thoughts off Him, we can get scared and forget that He is always there to help us. When you're facing hard things, you can know that Jesus is with you. Keep your attention on Him, and He will help you. —T.M.

READ MORE

Read Luke 8:22–25 to learn about another time Jesus rescued the disciples on the water.

FUN FACT

The Dead Sea lies on the border of Israel and Jordan. It is one of the saltiest bodies of water in the world. Because of how salty the Dead Sea is, people float very easily— but they can't walk on it!

Waiting for Good Things

The LORD is good to those who wait for him, to anyone who seeks help from him.

LAMENTATIONS 3:25 GW

"Good things come to those who wait" is a common saying that has been popular for many years. It reminds us of the importance of being patient.

God promised that Abraham would be the father of a great nation. He told Abraham to go outside and look at the sky. "There are so many stars you cannot count them," God said to Abraham. "In the same way, your descendants will be too many to count."

Abraham was about seventy-five years old when God promised to give him and his wife, Sarah, a son. But Abraham and Sarah waited another twenty-five years before their child was born! Abraham was one hundred years old and Sarah was ninety when they had their baby. His name was Isaac.

Kids have to wait for good things too. You have to wait for special days like your birthday or Christmas. You have to wait for your permanent teeth to grow in! Have you ever had to wait for a visit from your grandma and grandpa? It can be hard to wait, but good things come to those who wait.

I will wait for good things.

God is pleased when you wait patiently for good things. You don't have to wait for His love, because you already have that! But sometimes you have to wait for God to work out His plans as you grow up. God's timing is always right, so you can trust Him as you wait for the things you hope for.

Always believe that God will show you the good things He has for you. Remember that God's good things are worth waiting for. —C.B.

FUN FACT

A mother elephant has to wait more than a year and a half for her baby to be born! It takes about ninety-five weeks for an unborn elephant to develop inside its mother. That's more than twice as long as it takes for a human baby.

READ MORE

What is the greatest thing that Christians wait for?
Read John 14:1–3 to find out.

Say Thank You

Think of all the times you could say thank you. When someone gives you a gift, saying thank you is the right thing to do. You should also say thank you when someone pays you a compliment or helps you out. Do you remember to say thank you to your mom or dad for making a delicious dinner? Do you thank your grandma when she sends you a birthday card? When you pray, do you thank God for your home and your family? When you say thank you, it shows that you are grateful.

Give thanks no matter what happens. God wants you to thank him because you believe in Christ Jesus.

1 THESSALONIANS 5:18 NIRV

It's easy to be thankful for good things. But the Bible tells us to be thankful all the time—no matter what! Bad things can happen in anyone's life. People we love get sick. Friends move away. Parents can lose their jobs. We don't have to be thankful for the bad things themselves, but we can be thankful that God is with us during our hard times.

I will thank God all the time.

Anyone who believes in Jesus is a child of God. Good parents don't want to see their children sad or hurt, and God doesn't want that either. He wants you to depend on Him to help you through bad times. No matter what happens, you can be thankful that you have a God who loves you and cares about everything that happens in your life.

In good times and bad times, say thank you to God for loving you. —C.B.

READ MORE

Read Psalm 118:28–29.
Why should we give thanks to God?

FUN FACT

"Thanks" is the most popular one-word message typed on mobile phones. "Thank you" is the most popular two-word message!

> "If a man has a hundred sheep and one of them gets lost, what will he do? Won't he leave the ninety-nine others in the wilderness and go to search for the one that is lost until he finds it?"
>
> LUKE 15:4 NLT

The Lost Sheep

If you have a pet, you know how you would feel if you lost it. You would stop everything you were doing and go out to find it. You wouldn't worry about how far away you had to look or how long it took. You'd keep looking until you found your pet. You'd do everything you could to get it back.

When Jesus taught lessons about the kingdom of God, He often used parables. One of Jesus' parables talks about losing a sheep.

Jesus told the story of a shepherd who had one hundred sheep. One of those sheep got lost, so the shepherd left the ninety-nine others to go find the one that was missing. When he found the lost sheep, the shepherd picked it up and carried it home. He was so happy to find his sheep, he invited his friends and family to celebrate with him.

Jesus wants everyone to follow Him.

Jesus told this story to show how God feels about His people. God loves everyone—even the people who run away from Him. God will look for lost people just like the shepherd searched for his lost sheep. And when someone turns to God and becomes a Christian, there is much celebrating in heaven!

If you ever know someone who is running away from God, pray for that person. Always remember that God wants everyone to become a Christian. —T.M.

FUN FACT

The American Society for the Prevention of Cruelty to Animals did a study on dogs and cats that are lost. It learned that more than eight of ten lost pets are found again!

READ MORE

Jesus told another parable about something that was lost and found. Do you know what it was? Find out in Luke 15:8–10.

All Over the World

Did you know that when you wake up in the morning, other kids are getting ready for bed? It can be morning in one part of the world and nighttime on the other side of the earth. So when you're getting ready for bed at night, other kids are just starting their day. As the sun is setting in the sky where you live, it is rising someplace else.

> From where the sun rises to where the sun sets, the name of the LORD should be praised.
>
> **PSALM 113:3 GW**

It seems like the sun circles the earth, but it's the other way around. The earth "revolves"—or goes around—the sun, one time each year. But the earth also "rotates"—or spins—making one complete turn every day. As the earth revolves and rotates, the sun shines on different parts of the world.

I will praise the name of the Lord.

The Bible verse for today says that God's name should be praised from wherever the sun rises to wherever the sun sets. That means everywhere. And it means all the time.

God is so great—He is the one who created the sun and the earth and the heavens. He's the one who put the moon and the stars in the sky. He created the planets and set them in motion. God is the only one who could have done that.

The whole universe shows the glory and greatness of God. He is worthy of our praise. Everyone, everywhere, at every time can praise the name of the Lord. —C.B.

FUN FACT

It takes the earth a little more than 365 days to go around the sun. Each year actually takes an extra six hours. That's why, every four years, we add a "leap day"—February 29— to the calendar.

READ MORE

Read Psalm 113:1–6.
How great is God's glory?

SCRIPTURE PERMISSIONS

ABOUT THE AUTHORS

Crystal Bowman is a bestselling, award-winning author of more than eighty books for children including *The One Year Book of Devotions for Preschoolers*, *My Grandma and Me*, and *J Is for Jesus*. She also writes lyrics for children's piano music and stories for *Clubhouse Jr.* magazine. She is a mentor and speaker for MOPS (Mothers of Preschoolers) and teaches workshops at writers' conferences. She enjoys writing books for kids of all ages and wants them to know that God loves them and cares about them very much. Crystal is a mother and grandmother. She and her husband live in Florida where she likes to walk on the beach.

Teri McKinley grew up in the world of publishing, attending book signings and book conventions with her mother, Crystal Bowman. She began writing stories in elementary school and her love for writing grew in college while attending Baylor University. In addition to writing greeting cards for Discovery House Publishers and articles for national magazines, Teri has co-authored several books including *M Is for Manger* and *My Mama and Me*. She has a master's degree in interior design from Arizona State University and enjoys mentoring college students. Teri and her husband live in Texas.

Illustrator **Luke Flowers** spent countless childhood hours drawing sports heroes and comics at his grandfather's drawing desk. His love of art led him to Rocky Mountain College of Art and Design, where he earned a BFA in illustration. After ten years working for Young Life in the Creative Services Department, he launched Luke Flowers Creative, a company that seeks to "bring the illumination of imagination" to every project. Luke has won fourteen gold and silver Addy Awards for illustration and design.

HIS DAILY WISDOM.

HIS DAILY ADVENTURE.